HAPPY FAMILIES

An old game with new faces

Edited by Richard Cohen

With a preface by John Cleese

WITH FAMILIES BY:

Alex (Charles Peattie and Russell Taylor), Steve Bell,
Quentin Blake, Raymond Briggs, Peter Cross, Barry Fantoni,
James Ferguson, Fluck and Law, Nicholas Garland,
Charles Griffin, Martin Honeysett, John Jensen, Gray Jolliffe,
Larry, Sue Macartney-Snape, Matt, William Rushton,
Posy Simmonds, Trog *and* Lucy Willis

AND TEXTS BY:

Terence Blacker, Craig Brown, Alan Coren,
William Donaldson, Gavin Ewart, Valerie Grove,
Simon Hoggart, Terry Jones, Dillie Keane, Frank Keating,
Mark Lawson, Frank Muir, Stephen Pile, David Stafford,
D. J. Taylor, Sue Townsend, Fay Weldon, John Wells,
Roger Woddis *and* Victoria Wood

Methuen

The editor would like to acknowledge the help and kindness of both
John Jaques and Son and Gibson Games in the research for this book
and for the permission to publish it.

First published in Great Britain in 1992
by Methuen
an imprint of Reed Consumer Books Ltd
Michelin House, 81 Fulham Road, London SW3 6RB
and Auckland, Melbourne, Singapore and Toronto

All those who have contributed either pictures or words to HAPPY
FAMILIES have done so without payment. The royalties for the book will
be divided equally between the Russell Project and the Marilyn Monroe
Children's Fund.

A set of fifty-two playing cards featuring thirteen of the families in the
book has been published simultaneously by Waddington's Games Ltd.

Book designed by Katy Hepburn

ISBN 0 413 67010 4
A CIP catalogue record for this book
is available at the British Library

Typeset by Rowland Phototypesetting Ltd
Bury St Edmunds, Suffolk
Printed in Great Britain by
BPCC Hazells Ltd

CONTENTS

iv

PREFACE

by John Cleese MBE (pending)

I'd like to start by saying that this book is an extremely significant attempt to convey important information about children in an entertaining and, indeed, exciting way, and it is a great privilege for me to have been asked to write this preface to it. Actually, it isn't at all, but if you write an opening like the one above nobody bothers to read on, so at least I can continue this piece safe in the knowledge that the remaining ninety per cent of it will never be read. So, my favourite first names for chickens are: Tamara; Joy; Janice; Melanie; Hermann; Betty and Dobbin. The best results with rhubarb crumble are obtained if you frighten the rhubarb before frying it. Mary Queen of Scots was not beheaded; she was killed in the Blitz, by a hyperpatriotic fire warden. The reason Americans talk the way they do is that their tongues are too big. I'd better just write something else sensible and worthy in case anybody skims the beginning of the second paragraph. . . .

One big step forward that our society has taken in the past few years is that nowadays there are few people who do not know and appreciate that without any question childhood is a vulnerable time. Especially for children. Actually, why *is* there all this fuss about childhood? It's a doddle compared with your fifties when you can't hear or see properly any more, and bits of your body start dropping off and you have to carry lots of equipment round with you in order to function at all. Thank God I had hair transplants and got my teeth capped when I did. My next show should carry the credit, 'John Cleese appears by arrangement with European surgery.' But do we hear a word about middle-age deprivation? Not a sausage. The only thing sociologists and psychologists and colour supplement journalists and other people with clipboards and facial hair are interested in is deprived *children*. My parents never lavished on me what all the other children in Bevin Avenue got plenty of, i.e. deprivation. In fact, as a result, they did deprive me of the chance to be really interesting. So growing up without a firm grounding in deprivation I have been continually snubbed by every serious researcher in every branch of psycho-social science, behavioural and cognitive therapy, transactional analysis and primal retrogressive sublimation, even when I show them my bad knee and my bunion. Oops. Another new paragraph coming up.

In conclusion, I do urge you most strongly to put your hand in your pocket to purchase this outstanding, entertaining, informative, thought-provoking and, indeed, controversial publication. And if anybody did read all this by accident, I'm sorry if it's in bad taste, but at least I *did* write it and miss the first half of the football, which is something, though I suppose not enough to get me a complete honour. To get one of those, say an MBE, I'd guess you'd have to do four or five prefaces, at least. Either that, or give a couple of thou to the Tories. Which is a lot quicker, come to think of it, so I'll do that and forget about doing any more prefaces in future.

INTRODUCTION

'Happy Families' was commissioned by the games-making firm John Jaques in 1851, in time for the Great Exhibition, from John Tenniel, later Sir John, the chief cartoonist of *Punch*. Jaques as a company had been started in 1795, and as such is the oldest manufacturer of sports equipment in the world, particularly famous for its croquet sets. It was also one of the first games-makers in England to market card games seriously.

Before 1851, games in which players collected sets of four cards were common, the idea possibly taken from early German models. For some time such card games were called, simply, 'Quartets', although a version popular in the States dating from the 1830s was titled 'Authors'. Another set of Happy Families, 'John Bull', was on the market before Tenniel's families and several other versions predate it. Once Jaques's Happy Families established itself, several others were rushed on to the market, for copyright reasons given such names as 'Merry Families', 'Jovial Families' and 'Cheery Families'. Meanwhile, the Jaques version went from strength to strength, while the firm itself went on to make 'Tiddly-Winks', 'Ludo' and 'Snakes and Ladders'. In 1890, they invented and marketed 'Gossima', a game whose name was soon changed to 'Ping-Pong'. Launched through Hamley's in Regent Street, the game was an immediate success, and by 1920 was being played competitively. The name Ping-Pong, however, was regarded as dubiously as Gossima, and soon the game was re-christened 'Table Tennis'.

As for Tenniel's original illustrations for Happy Families,

he began with eleven families – forty-four cards in all. Ten years later, he drew his famous illustrations for *Alice in Wonderland* using both a more refined style and an even greater inventiveness. Tenniel had been commissioned personally by Lewis Carroll (the Reverend Charles Dodgson), whose last pocket-notebook (he died in 1898) contained the entry 'John Jaques & Son, Games and Puzzles'. Nineteen years later, Carroll's niece Irene Dodgson married John Jaques III, whose first wife had died in 1902. Before her marriage Irene had been employed by the firm as an artist and during the First World War her husband asked her to draw an additional family, as it was felt that two half-sized packs would be more convenient and more saleable than the full one. As forty-four cards could not be made into two equal half packs a new family of Mr Mug the Milkman was added to the originals; the game was only cut back to forty-four cards for costing reasons after the Second World War.

The war did more than increase costs. In 1941, during the Blitz, a large bomb fell on the firm's Hatton Garden factory, destroying it completely. For John Jaques and Company it was a disaster, their entire stock vanishing. However, a safe that had been kept at the top of the building and had fallen all the way through to the basement revealed inside it the charred remains of an old pattern book. This included the originals for all the firm's card games ('Counties of England' and so on) and one example of the Happy Families card game – Master Potts the Painter's Son. Later it was discovered that the plates for the game were intact – lodged at an out-of-London printer. Happy Families lived on.

Since John Tenniel's creations, however, there has never been any attempt by British artists to emulate his families. The 1851 lot are an artisan crowd – even the doctor, the only non-tradesman among them, is reduced to 'Mr' Dose. It is also a lower-middle-class, male-dominated group.

The 1992 set comes from the pens of twenty different artists, all of whom were asked to paint one family, the name and profession of which were their choice. To complement the eighty portraits, twenty writers have added their own descriptions of the families in the form of individual CVs, interviews, verse, reportage and memos to their secretary. Having set the project in motion, I was consulted only to avoid repetition, or occasionally on small matters of style. The result is both extremely funny and a telling demonstration of what twenty highly gifted artists think of 1990s Britain. It is Mrs Fax and Ms Rile who go to work, not their partners. Master Green is – not too obviously – adopted, while Master Steamer is the only member of his family with a recognised occupation: hooliganism. There is an aristocrat's family; also a down-and-out's. Jobs, in fact, characterise only a proportion of the families. Some are defined by enthusiasms, like the Scoutmaster's family, the TV addict's or the campaigner's. If Mr Green looks suspiciously like the recently retired leader of the Labour Party and the Greeds appear horribly familiar, no one could mistake the Poll family. And for Alex Masterley, the well-known cartoon paterfamilias of the *Daily Telegraph*, his creators had to come up with an intriguing way out of the fact that in their strip cartoon the Masterleys have only one child. Finally, Quentin Blake and Gray Jolliffe took the anarchic way out, in glorious style. What will those who buy the card game make of Mrs Nemo, all twenty stone of her, or Miss Einstein, Mr Trip's young mother? Yet all are recognisable families, joined by lifestyle, looks or shared enthusiasms, and are a fitting complement to the Grits, Potts, Dips, Buns, Doses, Soots, Bones, Chips, Cuts, Tapes and Blocks of the Great Exhibition of 1851.

Richard Cohen

THE SEEMLYS

Pictures by Posy Simmonds

The Reverend John Seemly is reasonably sure that he believes in God although he has learned, in the modern Church of England, to keep his public creed more general.

He was translated – which always makes Mrs Seemly giggle, thinking it makes him seem like the *Iliad* or something – to St Luke's in 1983. He arrived just after that year's election, in which he voted SDP, as he did again in 1987. He still remembers David Owen in his prayers although, in 1992, he voted Green. For – as he remarked in a recent sermon – God made the world in seven days and it sometimes seems as if man is trying to unmake it in the same period.

This is not to suggest that the Reverend Seemly regards the Genesis account as chronologically exact. However, his theology lecturer assured him that it was permissible to draw on generic Christian folklore for sermonic metaphor. Nor does the Reverend Seemly worry much about the veracity of the Virgin Birth. Personally, he agrees with a line he read in *God of the Ghettos*, a controversial work of modern theology: 'There are those in the Church who would argue that the ins and outs of single motherhood in Galilee back then count for little beside those of single motherhood in Gallowshiels now.'

St Luke's is a South London church, parts of which date from before the Reformation, although now the Reverend Seemly conducts joint services of worship there once a year with his Roman Catholic counterpart.

His parishioners are a 1990s British social stew.

Last week he buried an old dear who had worshipped at

St Luke's every Sunday, confinements excepted, since baptism there in 1898.

Next week he will baptise the child of two young types in advertising, who he suspects are not regular churchgoers (the father asked chirpily if it was all still in Latin) and who – when he demurred, remembering the Bishop's letter about Convenience Christians – wrote out to the Luke 2000 Fund a cheque for a twelfth of the Reverend Seemly's yearly stipend.

Every week he conducts a Sunday service constructed to reflect elements of the Pentecostal practices of his West Indian contingent: he was particularly happy with a rap version of 'Jerusalem' performed by his parish youth group.

And every day, it sometimes seems, he is on the telephone to a benefit office or a job centre or a bed-and-breakfast hostel, trying to intervene between bureaucracy and his parishioners' daily bread, as he put it in a letter to the *Guardian*, which the paper apologised for regrettably having no room to print.

For the poor of the parish, Mrs Rosemary Seemly – Rosie to those that know her – runs regular jumble sales. From the bundles that come in, she regularly removes some of the middle-decent garments – it would be wrong, she feels, to steal the cream – for her own family. The root of all evil has established only very shallow roots indeed around the Seemlys. John even donates money to charity although, as Rosemary has gently pointed out, the Seemlys could reasonably apply for such status themselves. In the end, Mrs Seemly thinks a vicar is probably just a social worker with a home thrown in – God, to her, is merely the expression of a human hope. But she does believe in Good and suspects that her husband is a representation of it.

Sometimes she understands why the Catholic Church

St LUKE's
Confirmation
Workshop

THE REVEREND SEEMLY
the vicar

MRS SEEMLY
the vicar's wife

MISS SEEMLY
the vicar's daughter

MASTER SEEMLY
the vicar's son

forbids its clergy to reproduce, for Good is not necessarily genetic and it would be unfortunate – not to mention bad for business – if a cleric spawned Satan. She does not feel that she and John have quite done that but Eve, aged ten, and baby Zikky (Ezekiel, as he was baptised) would try the patience of those many saints – variously boiled, raped and mutilated for God – to whom her husband's place of work is dedicated.

Eve, named by her husband with a metaphorical rather than fundamentalist nod to the Creation story, has the kind of well-scrubbed smugness which Mrs Seemly associates with Christians of the kind she and John are sometimes unlucky enough to meet on retreats. Eve has started to talk of 'pagans' and 'left-footers', which she must have picked up at school, because John has taught her that the various existing religions are just like different haircuts or languages: each a product of a particular culture or a valid individual choice. His daughter, though, goes round thundering: 'Either you are for me or against me.' Eve has also, some-how, heard of 'hell', which her father will not have men-tioned in the house; or, indeed, in the church.

Rosie reassures her husband that children always rebel against their parents' views and that, therefore, a modern vicar in the C of E will logically produce a daughter who believes the whole lot with Old Testament zeal. But the vicar's wife also remembers how she and her friends used to persecute the Christians at university, and hopes that Eve will fall before she gets there.

There are signs that she might. The senior Seemlys waste an hour a day stalking the house looking for the left-on television or radio they are convinced they can hear. It is, however, only the ghostly overflow from Eve's Walkman.

Rosie, despite being secretly encouraged by the signs of

her daughter's reversion to childhood normality, worries about the choice of music it involves. The cassettes Eve ceaselessly replays feature Madonna. Mrs Seemly has raised this matter with her husband.

'She's too young for it, John . . .'

'Oh, I don't know. I overheard a phrase the other day from one of them: "Like the Virgin". While one questions the, ah, literal interpretation, the use in popular entertainment of shared Christian folklore . . .'

'Like *a* virgin, John. That's what the song is . . .'

'Well, chastity, even in the modern world, is as valid a means of expression as . . .'

She abandons her latest attempt to expose him to the modern world. At least baby Zikky is less difficult. He has become a mascot for the lady geriatrics of the parish. The only problem is his zeal for eating; it is now clear how he has occupied himself when his mother dumps him in the aisle while flower-arranging the church. The hymnals are nibbled, the prayer books missing half-moon shapes of paper from their margins. The congregation suspect mice and have suggested poison. Only the Seemlys know the truth.

Mark Lawson

THE CAMPS

Pictures by Peter Cross

Some biographical notes as an aid to the compilers of the new edition of the Dictionary of National Biography.

Mr Camp the Scoutmaster

Mr 'Catterick' Camp's father was a military man who had served with no distinction whatsoever in the Army Catering Corps as an instructor in porridge-burning. Unlike his pretty son Catterick, he was an unlovely man, poor, nasty, brutish and short. But he married money. Catterick Camp's mother was a plump widow smelling of lavender and five-pound notes who had suddenly acquired a taste for rough trade. Catterick inherited little from his father except a penchant for wearing a uniform, which resulted in the lad joining, at one time or another, the Boys Brigade, the Salvation Army, the Boy Scouts, the Royal Corps of Commissionaires and the Garrick Club (for the beautiful club tie). Catterick Camp is not a muscular man like his father; his facial muscles are so feeble that to keep his unnecessary monocle in place he pretends to be saluting and presses the monocle against his nose with his fingertips. 'Catty', as Mr Camp is called without affection, has three interests in life: anointing his exquisite moustache hourly with a fingerful of *Pomade Hongroise*, polishing his boots with a pink silk hanky and trying to practise a ballet step while blowing his Scout's whistle at the same time.

Mrs Camp the Scoutmaster's wife

Mr Camp's wife Semolina was born in magnificent Luton Hall, a stately home so ancient that parts of the west wing go back as far as the Airport Departure Lounge. The future Mrs Camp was the eighth niece of the fourteenth Duke of Luton (or the fourteenth niece of the eighth Duke – it was difficult to be certain with all those winding corridors). In a glossy magazine her marriage to Mr Camp was called the Wedding of the Year by a semi-illiterate lady journalist but it was a reasonable comment given that nobody could conceive why Semolina would want to marry Mr Camp, or vice versa (although friends noticed that Mr Camp was taken suddenly rich after a meeting with the Duke just before the engagement). Semolina is notoriously peculiar but this does not matter as she is a member of the aristocracy and so it hardly shows and she gets away with being called 'eccentric'. (Only high-born or rich people are 'eccentric'; ordinary folk are 'barmy'.) Mrs Camp is a designer. Her recent inspirations include a pay-and-display parking meter for camp-sites which gives the wrong change and makes a fortune for the camp-site manager; a pale green portable lavatory camouflaged as a caravan; a combination shirt-and-bell-tent for ladies who love rain on their faces but hate wet feet; a Swiss Army knife permanently open so that fingernails are not broken trying to get at a blade; and spotted knickers trimmed with elastic lace so strong that the flow of blood is stopped and the legs go an interesting shade of white. Her hobby is wearing her husband's monocle.

Miss Camp the Scoutmaster's daughter

Miss Camp was an unwanted child. Mrs Camp wanted a boy and Mr Camp wanted a ride-on lawnmower so both were disappointed and did not speak to Miss Camp for the first twenty years of her life. In fact they were not able to speak to her on many occasions later because, through lack of interest, they had forgotten to christen her. She grew up a proud,

MR CAMP
the Scoutmaster

MRS CAMP
the Scoutmaster's wife

MISS CAMP
the Scoutmaster's daughter

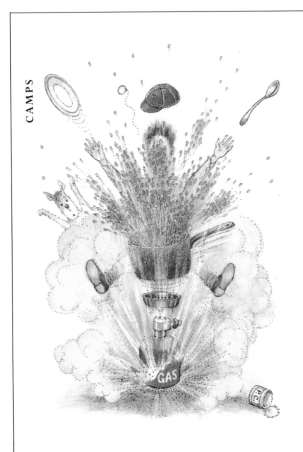

MASTER CAMP
the Scoutmaster's son

quiet girl, given to wearing long, boring brown skirts, eating jam tarts and blowing on an old police whistle which her father found in a puddle and gave her for her twenty-first birthday. Miss Camp is a gifted girl. She can tell the direction of the wind just by wetting her little finger and noting which side is going cold but she has made no attempt to use this remarkable gift to carve out a career. Instead she finds heart's-ease being alone with just an old patched tent and a bottle of gin disguised as barbecue-lighting fluid. She drinks the gin from a teacup because she heard that this was how Marlene Dietrich drank it in a film with Claudette Colbert. For fun, and because she knows how much he hates it, she steals and effortlessly wears Mr Camp's monocle.

Master Camp the Scoutmaster's son

Master 'Butch' Camp, a lone and tragic figure, seemed out of step with life throughout the pitifully little of it he was permitted by Fate to live. His doting mother cherished him from babyhood, warming the *Dom Perignon '27* to blood heat before pouring it into the font for his christening, chewing each forkful of his food for him before spooning it into his little mouth, and sending him to a Scottish public school which was the very antithesis of rough Gordunstoun. The school was called Fetish. The boys did not play violent games like Rugby but practised free-flow Grecian dancing in the manner of Isadora Duncan and played 25-a-side soccer with a shiny black rubber ball. Young Camp hated every minute of it. He came bottom in macramé and needlework and was smacked hard on the wrist by the headmaster for felling the games mistress with a head butt. The unavoidable fact was that young Camp had turned out to be a thug. He was finally dismissed from Fetish for setting fire to the school during prayers and running away, or rather joy-riding away in a stolen Ferrari. His father, Mr Camp, then devoted a great deal of his time to sorting out his wayward heir, a good half an hour whilst waiting for *Antiques Roadshow* to begin on television, and he unselfishly gave the lad his old Cubs uniform and cap. But all the time Master Camp was plotting revenge on his parents. Knowing their passion for eating Heinz baked beans under canvas, he devised a method of booby-trapping their Calor-gas camping stove. But just as he was adjusting the detonator, the whole fiendish device blew up in his face with a terrific bang. He had asked two friends to come with him, to share the blame if he was caught, but they had refused. So he went off all by himself. The only bit left of Master Camp was the mangled wreckage of his father's monocle which he was going to pawn to buy a share in a lorry going to Bangkok.

Frank Muir

P.S. 'Scamp', the Camp family's lovable dog, is not a lovable dog. He is a transvestite cat.

THE POLLS
Pictures by Trog

Of course, no real politician's family would ever look like the characters in Trog's drawings; what household could cope with four such monstrous egos? Though one feels one does know the families that such as these possess: Mark Thatcher, the mysterious, saturnine, offensive businessman is, these days, almost as well known as his mother. Sister Carol is the kinder, gentler face of Thatcherism. In anyone else, failure to pay the poll tax would appear an act of grim filial rebellion; in her it seemed agreeably scatterbrained.

I feel I know Mrs Currie's family from seeing them in television programmes, and later from encountering her husband Ray in a libel court, where she was defending herself against a charge of exploiting her family for publicity purposes. Ted Heath never had a family of his own, and I suspect has suffered as a result. Ray Currie once memorably said that at the end of a long hard day it was somehow difficult to get terrifically interested in the minutiae of House of Commons politics; such mild disdain is a useful corrective for politicians, who are otherwise liable to imagine that what they do actually matters. This in turn leads to brooding and a lack of proportion, something which a barking dog, a leaking roof and a child who wants to recite the whole of the poem she learned at school that day quickly restores.

But then being a member of a politician's family is not a job I would wish on anyone. It's arduous. Tory wives in particular are still expected to turn up at selection meetings exhibiting charm, loyalty and sensible Jaeger clothing. Once their husbands are selected they have to be their vicars on earth, attending coffee mornings, speaking in their absence and opening ward fund-raising fêtes. Given that MPs are, if not underpaid, at least paid much less than they could earn in business or the law, a wife may have to act as his Commons secretary as well, simply to bring in a second income to help pay for the second home.

If she happens to be fond of her husband, things get worse. Fine if the constituency is in or near London. If it isn't, the husband must commute on a weekly basis or else drag the family away from the town, the streets, the friends, the schools and the relatives they may have known all their lives. A precious weekend saved for a family outing can be wrecked by an importunate constituency chairman phoning to demand the MP's presence for a Saturday evening speech or a Sunday lunch. Some MPs can ignore this, but not those in marginal seats or those threatened by ambitious rivals from the same party.

Being bold enough to resist the pressure doesn't always help. Sir Christopher Soames tried to get the Tory nomination for Honiton and was asked whether, if selected, he would live in the constituency. 'Live? Live?' he roared. 'Surely nobody *lives* here?' He didn't get the seat.

If a wife doesn't play the game and refuses to turn up, there may be a whispering campaign against her. There are plenty of unreconstructed constituency parties on both sides whose members take a very dim view of persons of the female persuasion who have their own careers – which is one reason why there are so few women MPs. Some are loyal on a personal level only. I know a Tory wife who loves her husband so much that she refuses to be registered in his constituency, since she has no wish either to vote against him or to vote for the Conservatives.

A hard-working MP – and they do exist in plenty, whatever the cliché may hold – might see almost nothing of his

MR POLL
the politician

MRS POLL
the politician's wife

MISS POLL
the politician's daughter

MASTER POLL
the politician's son

family for four days a week or even more. Committees meet in the morning, the House sits after lunch and rarely rises much before 11 pm. An MP won't spend too much time in the Chamber listening to other MPs speak, but there are meetings to attend, letters to answer, constituency problems to tackle, dinners to scoff and conspiracies to hatch.

There's a pattern which is terribly familiar for some MPs. A friend of mine suffered from the syndrome. His constituency was 250 miles from London. The family decided to stay there. He was thrilled to become parliamentary private secretary to a very important minister, so that even when the House wasn't sitting he was away in Europe or America or Moscow, or just carrying the minister's bags round *his* constituency. Meanwhile the wife, bored to distraction, met up with an old boyfriend from school. Before long, he was taking the kids to the zoo or turning up for drinks after they were in bed. . . . My friend was shattered by the divorce; in his excitement and ambitious delight he had simply not seen it coming.

Life can be dangerous too. Several MPs have now been murdered by the IRA. The families of those who are at risk are constantly watched over by Special Branch. They are obliged to vary the times they take their children to school and the routes they use. They must use a mirror device to look under the car every morning. Some even have panic buttons round their necks, which send a distress signal to the nearest police station.

And life in the midst of publicity can be shattering. The public eye gazes unblinkingly every day of the year. Every politician, even the most obscure and lazy back-bencher, has some story about their family being wounded. 'Why is that man on the radio saying nasty things about my daddy?' might seem a winsome remark, unless it was your little girl who was making it. One prominent Labour politician found his young son in tears over the Sunday papers one weekend. 'Why do they write these awful things about you?' he asked. The MP realised with a shock that it is impossible to grow a thick skin for someone else.

Smoking bimbos play less of a part in political life than is often realised. Where would they go? Labour MPs tend to share cheap flats with people who know their wives. Even Tories are busy, and in my experience most people who are interested in sexual dalliance are not interested in standing outside factory gates at 7 am touting for votes or spending their evenings addressing crowds of eight people in draughty church halls. This may be one of the few consolations a political wife can have.

Simon Hoggart

THE MASTERLEYS

Pictures by Alex
(Charles Peattie and Russell Taylor)

Mr Masterley the corporate financier

Happy *what*? Oh Christ, I forgot all about the Happy Families project. Take down a memo on my private life, will you, Julie?

1. Happiness. When your working day is spent keeping a few dozen corporate balls in the air, there's precious little time for scratching your bum and wondering about 'happiness', whatever that may be. My job, at which I work bloody hard, by the way, provides a fair bit of contentment – 425,000 little units of contentment last year, including bonuses. (*Julie, check with Clive on whether this should be scaled down for the Concerned Nineties Reader*).

2. Home life. Sure, that has its place too. The very first thing I do when I get home is to check how Christopher's getting on at school and with his (*Ring Mrs Masterley and find out what instrument he's on will you, Julie?*) And when my wife's at one of her evening classes (*While you're at it, ask her what course she's on at the moment. Self-Assertiveness, probably. Or maybe Martial Arts*), I spend quality time with Chris, talking through his attainment goals for the coming year. I'm proud of the little bastard.

3. Summary. In a word – work hard, play hard. Maybe that sounds smug. I make no apologies. In many ways, I have the simple needs of an old-fashioned family man – money, job, home, son, and a young secretary who accompanies me on business trips in return for £25,000 and 100% bonus. (*That was a joke, Julie – I don't think we count as a Happy Family, do you?*)

At the end of the day, you take out of life what you put in. (*Very funny, love, just go and type the bloody thing up.*)

Mrs Masterley the corporate financier's wife

Oh, you don't want to know anything about me. I'm sure Alex has told you all about the Masterley home life – on which he's such an expert, of course. Give you the 'just an old-fashioned family man' line, did he? I thought so.

This morning Julie, the blonde of the moment, rang to ask me what instrument is your son playing, Mrs Masterley? Clarinet? Lovelee. Oh, and what evening class are you attending right now, Mrs Masterley? Lovelee. I wonder if that's what she says to Alex when they're on their business trips together. Ooh, Mr Masterley, *lovelee*.

Well, you'll find my home life absolutely fascinating. There's taking Christopher to and from school, clarinet lessons and tennis coaching. There are dinner parties for Alex's friends. There's the three afternoons a week I spend doing charity work at the local Oxfam shop. Then there's Dorothea, our daily, to sort out and the cottage in the Cotswolds which gets burgled at least once a month. I'm in charge of holidays, of course. Apart from that, I just sit at home, watching television, eating chocolate, waiting for the menopause.

Ah yes, my evening classes. If you must know, I go out to the cinema once a week – by myself. Sometimes I sit there watching Arnold Schwarzenegger or whoever, tears just coursing down my face. Silly, isn't it? I've got a husband who hardly recognises me and a son who actually *wants* to go to boarding school. And where do I fit into all this? I'd have an affair if I didn't think it would involve yet another bloody male making demands on me.

26

MR MASTERLEY
the corporate financier

MRS MASTERLEY
the corporate financier's wife

MASTER MASTERLEY
the corporate financier's son

MASTERLEYS

BABY MASTERLEY
(planned for the tax year after next)

Christopher Masterley the corporate financier's son

I give this marriage two years, frankly. Dad's given up on the family – you've heard of executive burn-out; he's got domestic burn-out. I merely have to *look* at Mum and she bursts into tears. When I told her that I had christened my teddy Dow Jones, it was monsoon time! Talk about walking on egg-shells.

Fortunately I'll be out of here pretty soon. Next year I go to Hawtreys, a fairly decent sort of prep school, so I'm told. 1998, it's Eton. I'll probably bum around India on a motor-bike to get a taste of real life before barrelling my way through the good old Harvard Business School, then on-wards and upwards to my first million.

One thing's for sure. I'm not going to turn into my father. Merchant banking? Too slow. A quick killing on the trading floor, then into brokerage. Tomorrow's sharks will make Dad's generation look like goldfish.

Baby Masterley

It messes you up for life, being a mistake. I'll be trouble from the unhappy moment I'm conceived. She will have come off the pill saying that she's messing up her body for nothing. He'll be in a spasm of guilt and self-loathing having just been dumped by Julie for a younger, richer man.

Ugh. That moment of conception. You don't want to know about it. They'll be angry. I'll be angry. I tell you, I'll be so pissed off that I'll fertilise that egg out of sheer spite.

I'll be a difficult baby, a diapered hooligan, the despair of child psychologists everywhere. They'll try discipline – I'll break it over their heads. They'll try leniency – I'll stretch it until it snaps . . . .

As I develop my uniquely psychotic personality, Mr and Mrs Masterley will find themselves united at last.

Exhausted, ageing, no longer buoyed up by money (you thought Black Monday was bad? Wait until you see 1995!), they'll just fade like an old photograph.

Christopher's self-esteem I'll regard as a long-term project. By the time he hits eighteen, he'll be so edgy, thanks to his little brother, that he'll be lucky to get a place at the local polytechnic. He'll make a wonderful social worker.

I quite like the idea of being a transvestite. At Mr and Mrs Masterley's silver wedding, I'll turn up in a sequinned cocktail dress and raise a glass (the first of many) to them and their scruffy, defeated older son.

I'll say, 'Here's to our happy family!'

Terence Blacker

THE STEAMERS

Pictures by Nicholas Garland

Master Steamer the football hooligan

I wouldn't have been near the place, let alone arrested, if it hadn't been for Dad. Nothing would have happened if Dad had come with me to the ground that Saturday like he said he was going to, but once she was there in the boozer I knew he wasn't going to drag himself away. Anyroad, he says, whether I'm going to the match or not I've got to take Maggie home first – that's our dog – and not to go the Boleyn way else she'll set on those German shepherds the police have got out for the match and tear them to pieces, har, har. He's always full of, you know, har-hars and sort-of pathetic jokes when he's pouring drinks down that Loretta. What sort of name's that to start with? Eyetie, is it? Anyroad, the night before, the Friday, Dad says why not meet him at some place down Plaistow and not to tell Mum – as per usual – and to wear my shirt with a collar, and he'd introduce me to someone who might do me a good turn, like, and, har, har, he said, further me education.

I'd been expecting this. I knew Loretta had a skinny bint 'cos I'd seen her helping out with the dresses in the market some weekends and Rainy Rainsford had said she might be skinny but she was a right goer, so I thought, why not? I told Mum I was going out with the fellers and got to this dark-lit downstairs gaff in Plaistow and there was Dad and Fatso and her daughter sitting at a table waiting for me, drinking wine. Well, I had a glass of the stuff and it was piss and I said I'd have a Black Label but Dad said they didn't sell beer in this sort of place, so why not take Bren – that was the skinny tart's name – up the road to the pub and have a couple of beers? He and his woman would join us later. Bren seemed keen enough but once we got outside in the car park she got all humpy and said she'd holler if I didn't lay off. Not on a first date, she said. They all say no at first, don't they? You know, Stop It, I Like It! Anyroad, in the end, although I had one arm round her, tight, she was struggling so much and her jeans was so tight at the top I couldn't get me other arm down them, that when she started to really holler I pushed her down on the ground, called her a slag, and went on up to the pub in disgust.

Next morning Dad gives me a bollocking once Mum had gone off to open the stall, but he couldn't say too much 'cos he knew I'd tell Mum about his tart. But a bit of advice, son, when it comes to bints, he says, don't get stuck straight in, he says, butter 'em up before touching 'em up, that's the secret. Anyway, he said he'd come down the Hammers with me in the afternoon for the last time – 'cos they're bound to go down, aren't they? Tell you the truth, I don't know why I bother any more – haven't had a decent ruckus for a long time. Not since Leeds have gone straight, the poxy bastards. Anyroad, I was giving it one more match, but taking Maggie back to the flat first and down the market pretending to scare the Pakis by looking to let her off the lead, when I bump into two of the fellers and they start patting Maggie and saying, good girl and all that to her, and say they're not going to the Hammers no more, not ever, and they've got a much better idea for this afternoon for me and them. So off we go there and then . . . .

Mr Steamer the football hooligan's father
I blame myself totally. If I hadn't told him to take the dog Maggie home first, he'd have gone to the match. But I was on a promise with Loretta and when I go up her place there's

34

MASTER STEAMER
the football hooligan

MR STEAMER
the football hooligan's father

MRS STEAMER
the football hooligan's mother

MISS STEAMER
the football hooligan's sister

nowhere for the dog to be put except locked up in the kitchen. And Loretta took the hump when it bit the leg off her kitchen table that time. Anyroad, that's all by the by . . . . The boy's really gone and done it this time. I told him when we saw him in the cells on Saturday evening that he'd really gone and done it. How could you? I said. How could you do it to the poor girl? I can't tell you the blood and the cuts and that . . . .

Mrs Steamer the football hooligan's mother
He's a good boy deep down. Not that he exactly did it her himself, but like they say the feller who only guards the door in a gang-bang, well, he's just as in it up to here as the bastard who's actually caught with his trousers down. Once they showed him the photos of her injuries, he said, Oh Mum, and started crying again.

Miss Steamer the football hooligan's sister
The RSPCA feller agreed she's a lovely dog and if you treat Rotties right they treat you right. With all his football form, it'll be six months at least. Serves the little git right. Don't have a leg to stand on. As if he didn't know when those two fellers said, Let's take your Mags up Forest Gate for a promising little ruckus. Some out-of-bounds warehouse place. The poor girl didn't have no chance. Torn to bits by a pit-bull who'd been starved for months for this dogfighting. If the raid had been twenty seconds later, Mags would be dead, the RSPCA feller said.

Frank Keating

THE BOXES

Pictures by James Ferguson

Mr Box the down-and-out of Cardboard City

Mr Box's has been a success story. There was a time, in his days as an unemployed garbage collector, when he was a drain on society. He relied on the local council to provide his house, and he sponged off Social Security in order to provide for his children. But one day all that changed.

Mr Box was watching the TV (which he'd found on a skip in Upper Park Road) when a famous politician came on the screen and said, 'Get on yer bike!'

Immediately Mr Box went down to the public library (which in those days still had a few books on the shelves) and read the entire works of Milton Friedman. 'That's right!' he said. 'Market forces must be given complete freedom in which to operate, without government interference!' He realised that he and his dear ones were directly responsible for at least some of the distortions that currently disfigured the operation of the market economy in Britain today. 'If it weren't for us, my dears,' he explained, 'there would probably be many a family in Upper Park Road who could now be investing in a second freezer. We must become more self-reliant.'

Fortunately, Mr Box's new resolution was helped by several exciting events. First the council sold off their council houses and put the Box family into bed-and-breakfast accommodation. Then Social Security started refusing to pay out the huge amounts of money they had in the past. They tripled the number of forms Mr Box had to fill in and made it more difficult for him to claim anything. Finally Mr Box called his family together and proudly announced that they

MR BOX
the down-and-out of Cardboard City

MRS BOX
the down-and-out's wife

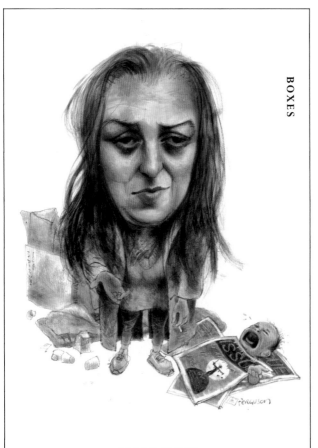

MISS BOX
the down-and-out's daughter

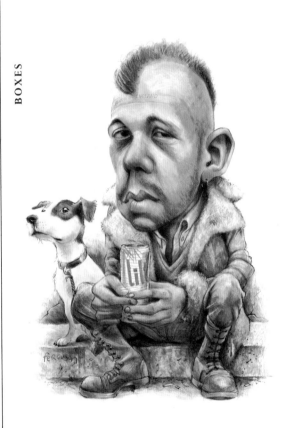

MASTER BOX
the down-and-out's son

were going independent. With a light heart he put his sandwiches in a handkerchief and set off on a new life of freedom, sleeping wherever he wanted, never having to work and unbothered by poll-tax collectors or anyone wanting his vote.

And that is how he still lives.

Mrs Box the down-and-out's wife

Mrs Box has never been the sort to settle down to the humdrum drudgery of married life. She married Mr Box out of a feeling of duty when she became pregnant, but never lost her taste for a freer lifestyle. Even the fun of trying to bring up two children on a weekly Social Security cheque couldn't replace the call of the open road.

So when they were finally thrown out of their council accommodation it was the fulfilment of a lifetime's ambition. Now she was truly free. All she needed was an old supermarket trolley and half a dozen bags. She wrapped her worldly goods up in newspaper and set off.

When you see her walking down the street, you would never imagine she had once been borne down by family cares, that once she had worked as a shorthand typist in a local merchant bank. When you see her rolled up in her newspapers, happily dozing in some shop doorway, surrounded by her bags and bric-à-brac, you would little think that one of those bags contains a bundle of photographs of a holiday in Margate she once had – with Danny Penrose, the one boy she'd really loved.

Miss Box the down-and-out's daughter

Miss Box never cared for life in the old house or, later, in the accommodation provided by the council. So she thanked the government with a full heart when it forced the local council to reduce its housing stock and her family found themselves kings of the road.

From her earliest years her ambition had been to be independent. The government made this dream come true by making it impossible for her to fall into the trap of working. As there wasn't any work, she never had to go through the humiliating experience of checking in from nine till five, or having to be polite to a greasy young man in a suit while he tried to put his hand in her blouse. No, Miss Box's life has always been fiercely her own.

Inside her sleeping bag she keeps a small notebook in which she writes down her experiences of life and the occasional poem. If she had been less fortunate she could perhaps have ended up as the editor of a women's magazine, or as the Middle East correspondent for the BBC. But the school where she was educated didn't have the money to waste on books or pens or paper.

Now she thanks God that she lives in a caring society – where people only smoke half their cigarette and you can find the longest stogies in the world.

Master Box the down-and-out's son
Sartorially the smartest of the whole Box family, Master Box is no less successful in his own way.

He left school at the unusually early age of nine and was educated thereafter at a variety of establishments for young gentlemen. Most of the proprietors are now serving their country in far-off places with romantic-sounding names such as 'Dartmoor' and 'Brixton'.

Master Box is a great supporter of Mrs Margaret Thatcher (even though she is no longer in government) because he admires the way she would never let anyone tell her what to do. He believes in the freedom of the individual and is intensely interested in politics. He reads the *Sun* and believes that the world is on the verge of a millenium (which indeed it is), in which all humanity will live together in peace and harmony along with their dogs, and where conflict will be confined to the football pitch, the terraces and the pubs surrounding the stadium for four or five hours afterwards.

His dream is to build a classless society – one in which there are no classes because there are no jobs. 'What's the point,' he remarks, 'of stuffing your head with rubbish about the Boer War or the invention of the steam engine, when they never ask you questions about those things on your Income Support form?'

Terry Jones

THE BUMS

Pictures by Steve Bell

Bernie Bum the builder

Bernie Bum the builder,
A man of massive frame,
Presents a view that is taboo,
But broadly fits his name.

The flesh that fills his denims
(There's more than meets the eye)
Evokes complaints from prudes and saints,
And cheers from passers-by.

Brenda Bum the builder's wife

Behold the burly Brenda,
A loyal builder's mate,
Her ample rump a mite too plump
To figure in the Tate.

If she were on the telly,
The show would run for weeks,
And she'd become the nation's Mum
When starring in *Twin Cheeks*.

MR BUM
the builder

MRS BUM
the builder's wife

MASTER BUM
the builder's son

MISS BUM
the builder's daughter

Billy Bum the builder's son

Although he's not a sailor,
He's master of his craft,
Which he displays as people gaze
On Billy Bum abaft.

He has, as all acknowledge,
A gift for laying bricks,
Though he'll confess has rather less
Success in laying chicks.

Bonny Bum the builder's daughter

When born they called her Bonny,
A name she bore with pride,
But she rebelled when schoolmates yelled,
'Hey, Bonny, where is Clyde?'

She hoped to be a gymnast,
Who stars on bars and rings;
Now people shriek and scaffolds creak,
Whenever Bonny swings.

Roger Woddis

THE GREENS

Pictures by Fluck and Law

As just one small family in the larger family of Mankind, we in the Green Family would rather you had not bought this book.

It may look attractive or 'amusing'. For ourselves, we can see that it is probably very 'funny' to look at snide caricatures of those of us who are doing our bit for the good of the environment. The book's proceeds may be going to a worthwhile, albeit human cause. But this book was once part of a great big living tree, and that tree has had to suffer and die so that you may be 'amused'.

Many woodland creatures will have been adversely affected by your action. This page alone was probably home to over sixty species of rare bug, none of which will have survived the rigours of pulping, printing, binding, transportation and being browsed through in a bookshop. If by any chance you come across a rare species of bug while enjoying this book, please, please give it a good home and educate it in Green Awareness.

We have agreed to participate in this massive bug genocide only for the greater cause of saving the planet. After seeing these 'humorous' portraits of us in action, many of you will have decided that you want to be like us. But perhaps you don't quite know how to set about it. We have thus compiled this handy cut-out-and-keep Green Family question-and-answer programme to set you on course.

Q: I am anxious to live a Green life. Does this preclude drinking wine?
Mr Green: Not at all. The Green Family drinks wine in

MR GREEN
the campaigner

GREENS

MRS GREEN
the campaigner's wife

MISS GREEN
the campaigner's daughter

GREENS

MASTER GREEN
the campaigner's son

moderation, causing little or no suffering to the planet. But do be sure to obey these three Green rules:

i) Make sure your wine is lead-free;

ii) Never drink wine out of a receptacle made of glass, paper or plastic;

iii) If you must drink wine, stick to the excellent non-alcoholic brands, and be sure to drink in the dark. Use of valuable electricity resources for so selfish an activity constitutes irresponsible citizenship, and cannot be sanctioned.

Q: The Green Family has a reputation for puritanism. Is this fair?

Mrs Green: Not at all. Obviously we say no to the conventionally-accepted wisdom that dictates that consumer durables add to the sum of human happiness, but we find many deeper pleasures in existing in harmony with our environment. As a family, we foregather on a regular basis to assert the joy of life in an environmentally friendly manner. We begin these sessions by simply breathing, thus relishing the pleasures of passive non-smoking. After a couple of hours of this, we include ourselves in a Green Awareness Game called 'Avoiding the Harmful Rays of the Sun', with everyone crouching in a darkened room with their eyes shut.

Another excellent game, specially designed to reduce the aural pollution of laughter from children, is the excellent 'Standing Still with your Mouth Shut'. Green children will grow to love this pastime, which involves virtually no damage whatsoever to the ozone layer. If they can also be encouraged to take only every second breath this will do much to help the earth's vastly depleted oxygen reserves. So let it never again be said that the Green Family doesn't know how to enjoy itself!

Q: We are thinking of throwing a dinner party just like the Green Family does. Advice, please, on how to greet our guests.

Ms Green: A Green Family dinner party is best described as an interactive self-awareness group socializing over an environment-friendly vegetable product in order to pursue Green issues among a like-minded peer-group for mutual help and Green advancement, and as such can be terrific fun. As your guests arrive, offer them a choice of rainwater or distilled tapwater. You will not have succumbed to the consumer-oriented lure of central heating and your guests may thus require something to, as it were, break the ice, so by all means keep a supply of axes ready.

Q: As devout Greens, we have set about redecorating our sitting-room. First, we removed all synthetic materials, as they are full of pollutants and environmentally unfriendly substances. This meant throwing out the lamps, sofas, cushions, paintings, television, etc. Then we got rid of all natural materials, as there has already been far too much destruction of our heritage of crops, woodland and animals. Out went the curtains, table, floorboards and carpets. We now have a bare room with no floor. Though we eschew the fripperies foisted on us by the pressures of multinational consumerism, we would like to cheer the room up a little. Any suggestions?

Master Green: Try whistling.

Craig Brown

THE CODS

Pictures by William Rushton

Mr Cod the comedian

Educated at Repton, Tristram Codrington studied Medi-
aeval Italian and Renaissance Glass with the intention of
entering a career in the Diplomatic Service.

Arriving at Cambridge in the afterglow of 'The Goodies',
Tristram found himself increasingly drawn to the glamorous
world of undergraduate revue. After playing several 'walk-
on' roles like Second Man in Waiting Room in the famous
'My Stoat Has Got Dandruff' sketch, he rose to become Road
Manager for a touring version of *Several Degrees Under*, a
satirical compilation of mime, slapstick and wry political
comment which sold out when it visited Moosejaw's Gem
Theater.

It was this experience that convinced Tristram his true
vocation lay in the realm of entertainment. He served two
years' hard apprenticeship with the Al-Badawi Gay Refuse
Collectors' Amateur Operatic Society of Stevenage; though
not a fully paid up member, he liked to quip, he would 'help
out when they were busy'. In 1978 he obtained provisional
membership of Equity.

Years of testing unemployment followed, during which
he 'stuck to his guns', always ready to appear, however
short the notice, at charity functions and friends' weddings.
His 'I Dreamt I Was One of the Queen's Corgis' monologue
was reviewed in *The Stage and Television Today*.

In 1986 Cod's real break came – he was asked to play
Straight Man to the BBC's Welsh-Language Breakfast TV's
chart-topping *Gwyn-y-Moron* (Maurice the Gerbil). He has
since enjoyed regular employment as a pub comedian. He is

best known for his voice-over endorsement of the Etna Sanitary Towel.

Mrs Cod the comedian's wife

Born Eleanor Theodora Mainwaring-Rubenstein, Mrs Cod was studying Household Economy in Cambridge when she met her husband. Marrying Cod was a decision she frequently regretted, and nowhere more movingly than in her privately published novel *Mr Mouse Comes Out to Play*.

It was not long before she struck out. Having dreamed of a career as a dancer, Eleanor was dogged by a weight problem. This effectively dished her chances of portraying Elvira in Mantovani's *I Piccolini di Wantage*, and was blamed by some for the semi-tragic accident, six months later, when she was lifted into the air as Donalda the Wild Duck in Brian Smith's *Avec Nous Le Deluge*, causing multiple injuries to her game South American partner, Oswaldo Fish, and serious structural damage to the revolving stage.

Undeterred, Eleanor threw herself with renewed energy into a one-woman aquatic version of *War and Peace*, set to *musique concrète*. Alas, poor attendances and the cost of shoring up the disused aircraft hangar in which she staged the show led to a nervous breakdown, a spell in intensive group therapy in California and a decision to release her two teenage children into the community.

It was on her return to the United Kingdom in the autumn of 1987 that she volunteered, 'as an exercise in conceptual art', to assist her husband in his cult routine *Just a Trifle!* This was to bring her within a whisker of being immortalised in extruded polystyrene in the *Guinness Wonderful World of Freaks*, sustaining as she did as many as two hundred facial custard pie attacks in the course of four minutes.

She is a keen Esther Rantzen fan, still plays prop forward

MR COD
the comedian

MRS COD
the comedian's wife

MASTER COD
the comedian's son

CODS

MISS COD
the comedian's daughter

for the Chingford Mature Ladies' Skunks and is active in social work. She is happiest in her favourite field of Cooking for the Disturbed.

Master Cod the comedian's son

At Bedales, Saffron Hairdryer Cod showed an interest in early music and embroidery. He soon formed a close friendship with the then captain of lacrosse, Giles Sweeting, who encouraged him in many different fields.

Launching out into the big world shortly before taking his GCSE, Saffron lived rough in London's West End before a government-subsidised Movement Course at Merton Polytechnic led to an opening at Cheltenham Ladies' College, where he taught elocution and deportment. But not for long. Ever a rolling stone, Saffron's restless genius led him through work as a waiter in Berlin, a breeze-block miner in Hungary and a needle-boiler in Amsterdam before he finally became official spokesman on Youth Opportunities at Conservative Party Central Office. Once there his boisterous good humour and wicked talent for mimicry at once endeared him to the then Mrs Thatcher.

It was seeing Ben Elton and Alexei Sayle in *Lilac Time* on television that inspired him to take up alternative comedy, and in particular the political monologue. The form, in Saffron's sensitive hands, is always charged with a deep sense of personal commitment, combined with a searing analysis of the contemporary political scene.

He is at present raising funds for a sponsored swim of the North Atlantic, no proportion of which will be given to charity.

Miss Cod the comedian's daughter

Compared as a toddler to the young Shirley Temple by her mother, and by her father to the older Edward Heath,

Samantha Yvonne Cod immediately made her mark in the Amateur Dramatic Society at Roedean Junior School with a string of successes. These included leading roles as King Lear, Othello and Vlad the Impaler. In all of them she displayed a radiant cheerfulness that won over the most reluctant audiences, and an energy that left her fellow-actors exhausted.

After school she immediately threw in her not inconsiderable lot with the Womens' Movement, and was one of the first to pitch her bell-tent at Greenham Common. A weight problem, inherited from her mother, was turned to unexpected advantage when she was chosen as the ideal candidate to breach the barbed wire at the American nuclear base.

Rolled forward on her side by the Militant Sisters with slowly increasing speed, she successfully flattened the perimeter fence and went on to wreck three American tanks and a coffee stall. Her exploit was recorded by Westward TV's evening magazine programme *Go West!* and she was picked as Big Woman of the Year by Jumbo Fashions of Swindon. She was also chosen to 'star' in the television commercials promoting the 'Greenham Common' range of Cuddly Stuffed Hippos in their familiar Barbour coats and woolly hats that subsequently became such a craze in the toyshops.

It was this television success that encouraged her to follow the rest of the family into showbusiness. Her childrens' books, notably *Pudgy the Helicopter Pilot*, a feminist view of the life and work of the Duchess of York, as well as her radio ventriloquist act with Sir Peter Porker the Chauvinist Pig, have made her a rival to Cilla Black in the affections of politically committed women everywhere.

John Wells

THE SNAPS

Pictures by John Jensen

Mr Snap the photographer

Described by the tabloid which employs him as GEOFF 'GEOFF' SNAP, 49, HUNKY SQUIRE OF FLAME-TRESSED EX-MODEL TRISH, FORMERLY 36:24:36, Mr Snap understandably hates the tabloid which employs him.

He always has. Once he dreamed of following Henri Cartier Bresson into the High Andes to capture the essential humanity of nonagenarian herdsfolk; once he dreamed of parachuting into Vietnam alongside Don McCullin to capture the essential inhumanity of war; once he dreamed of mincing in the footsteps of Cecil Beaton to capture 250k a year from *Vogue*; but while waiting for all this to happen he took a job as piggyback to the tabloid's ace paparazzo.

The job required Mr Snap to stand around in all weathers so that the ace paparazzo could climb onto his shoulders whenever a celebrity sped by; which meant that in the fullness of time Mr Snap himself became an ace paparazzo. He now wanders the *demi-monde* by day and night, hung with a dozen cameras each capable of intruding more intimately than the next, in the hope of bumping into celebrities furtively scuttling in ginger wigs from the side exits of cheap hotels and massage parlours.

Sozzled, as these days he more and more frequently is, he will weepily reveal his one remaining dream of getting a photograph into New York's Museum of Modern Art. This, however, is unlikely, given that all his work bears the unmistakable hallmark of wonky fuzziness which comes from being shot through a 600mm lens by a sleet-swept drunk standing on somebody's shoulders.

Mrs Snap the photographer's wife

Grey-tressed Trish, now 48:36:48, first came to prominence (as the tabloid which employed her never failed to describe it) by becoming its earliest nude pin-up in the great pioneering days of the late sixties when, her *balcon* sellotaped to perfection, Trish enchanted everyone who claimed to buy the paper for its peerless sports reporting.

Like Geoff, she too had her dreams, for which posing naked on a pogo stick in the company of a stuffed kitten was but the requisite prelude. Though those who had known her as Miss Cleethorpes had been led to believe that her true ambition was to work for world peace by opening a chain of chic boutiques catering to underprivileged children, Trish had in fact set her heart, or at least everything outside it, on becoming an international film star.

However, despite the fact that she managed to secure a walk-on role as a topless astrophysicist in *Carry On Up Venus,* her film career subsequently faltered when this brief part ended up on the cutting-room floor, a spot to which, it must be admitted, Trish was no stranger. Broke, she went back to work at the tabloid, but the disappointment had taken its toll, turning her, for consolation, towards compulsive eating. Soon, at eighteen stone, she could no longer commend herself to her former fans, and was given notice.

It was then that the gallant Geoff stepped in. By now the tabloid's ace paparazzo and in need of something solid to stand on in order to snap celebrities, he offered Trish the job. Inevitably, they married, since when she has frequently looked back.

Miss Snap the photographer's daughter

Samantha Snap, eighteen, photographed here by her father, has spoken to neither of her parents since becoming a

MR SNAP
the photographer

MRS SNAP
the photographer's wife

MISS SNAP
the photographer's daughter

MASTER SNAP
the photographer's son

member of SAP.

Sisterhood Against Photographers is committed to ending the degradation and exploitation of the female body, ideally by assassinating anyone involved in the pin-up trade and burning their corpses on a pyre of old tabloids but, where this is impractical (for example where they are providing you with room, board, clothes and a white Golf convertible), by destroying their credibility and livelihood.

It might be thought that this photograph of Samantha is merely evidence of how unaccustomed Geoff is to taking pictures when not standing on anyone, but this is not so. In fact, the snap was a perfectly acceptable portrait, showing the subject's entire head, before Samantha cropped the top off and sent it not only to Geoff's tabloid but to all its rivals, together with an anonymous note explaining that her father was now so drunk he could no longer be relied upon to snap anything.

Fortunately for Geoff, there has so far been no reaction, thanks to the recipients themselves being too drunk to read or sign anything – except, of course, one another's expenses.

Master Snap the photographer's son

Jason Snap, twelve, burns to follow in his father's footsteps, which is why he frequently takes his mother unawares by attempting to climb her.

His ambition is not driven, as might be assumed, either from pubescent ambitions of working with undraped colleagues on pogo sticks or from youth's predictably anarchic dreams of bringing down Cabinet Ministers or Royals by snapping them unawares from a nearby tree: Jason is besotted with kit. A product of the generation which has seen cameras replaced by systems, he loves handling the wondrous toys and their even more wondrous auxiliary gewgaws with which unscrupulous manufacturers, recognising an addiction when they see it, continue to flood the market, despite the fact that the true needs of 99.9% of the purchasers would be served by an old cigar-box with a pinhole in it.

Thus, if asked what he wants to be when he grows up, Jason Snap will cry: 'A photographer!' He does not understand that, if you want to be a photographer, growing up is the one thing that could disqualify you.

Alan Coren

THE RILES

Pictures by Raymond Briggs

Ms Rile the reformer put in time at an assertiveness training course, and so may appear intimidating to the outside world. But her heart is of gold. The course was necessary because when she presented herself as feminine and gentle, so many of her clients failed to pay their bills and she was subjected to a deal of sexual harassment. If she does not often smile, it is because she has an unemployed husband and two children to support, and goes home from work to shop, cook and housekeep. Her vital statistics – 42:32:40 – are Marks-and-Spencer norm for the female population as a whole. Ms Rile gained her plumbing certificates through a government retraining scheme for the unemployed, and is three times as good a plumber as most you will encounter. She has to be. Plumbing is on the whole a male preserve. If Ms Rile wishes to reform the world, it is not surprising. She has started with herself.

Mr Rile, Ms Rile the reformer's insignificant other, is so described by the neighbours, who drink lager and believe in 'traditional' values; that is to say, wife-beating and keeping pit bull-terriers, whom they encourage to foul the Riles' front garden. Mr Rile, who is out of work (the unemployed to the employed ratio in his area is 4 to 1), works hard at his body-building, the better to tackle the neighbours when they push lighted rags through the letterbox in the name of the values they espouse. He is a good father and likes to be at home with the children, which is just as well since so few child-care facilities are available for working mothers. He is a great moral support to his wife. It is not size that counts, as we all know; or only in the absence of affection.

Ms Rile (Junior), once an agreeable girl child, is now of indeterminate sex, as a result of drinking tapwater supplied by the local Water Board, following an incident in which liquid hospital waste containing an undue percentage of the male hormone testosterone was allowed to leak into the water supply. In order to preserve an appropriate level of 'investment funds', rusty pipes had not been replaced. The Board has apologised most sincerely but so far refuses to pay the Riles' compensation, arguing that there is no evidence that Ms Rile (Junior) is any different in her behavioural patterns from many a young girl today, who take admonitions in relation to 'safe sex' very seriously indeed. The lawsuit continues. Ms Rile (Junior), moreover, has taken it upon herself to defend her little family from attack by the neighbour's pit bull-terrier. She is very brave and does well at school.

Master Rile, the reformer's second child, is, like his sister Ms Rile (Junior), currently the subject of a long lawsuit. Friends of the Earth pay all legal fees, since the Rile family are on the breadline. The Riles live close to an Intensive Chicken Unit; young Master Rile, toddling in the little back garden, ingested oestrogen in sufficient quantity to distort his hormonal balance. He misses his mother who has no choice, the world being what it is, but to work long hours. It is to be hoped that his father will presently find employment, but even so these days it takes two incomes to keep one household going properly and it is unlikely, one way and another, that he will see much of his maternal parent during his childhood. But he is making great efforts to do without his comforter, poor little lad! He is a great joy to his parents.

Fay Weldon

MS RILE
the reformer

MR RILE
the reformer's insignificant other

MS RILE (JUNIOR)
the reformer's daughter

MASTER RILE
the reformer's son

THE DOOMS

Pictures by Martin Honeysett

Mr Doom came out of the swing door of the embalming room and sat down at the kitchen table. He didn't bother to remove his rubber apron: he had another corpse to prettify after tea.

Mrs Doom crashed out of the scullery with a plate piled with stale sandwiches left over from a funeral tea held the day before.

'Doom!' she shouted. 'You know the rules: no rubber gloves at table.'

Mr Doom sighed, peeled off his slimy gloves and laid them on the grey tablecloth next to his teacup and saucer. He winced and held his ears as Mrs Doom bellowed, 'Tea's ready!' to the children who were playing 'State Funerals' at the bottom of the garden.

Mr Doom looked at his wife's face. She was in a vicious mood all right. What had he done wrong? Nothing that he could think of: perhaps it was the weather? She was never comfortable on these sunny, bright June days. Like him, she preferred a nice gloomy February with a touch of mist about. He thought back with nostalgia to the days of his childhood when a fog was truly a fog.

'Anythink wrong, Mrs D?' he asked, as she cuffed the children to their seats at the table.

'Anythink wrong?' she mocked. 'Oh *no*, Doom, everythink is hunky dory, I'm over the bleedin' moon, as happy as a cowin' sandboy, a pig in shit couldn't be more 'appier than me.'

Mr Doom suspected that Mrs Doom was not telling the full truth. Perhaps it was the way she was pouring his tea, holding the teapot a good three feet above the table so that the scalding liquid splashed out of his cup and on to his face and hands. Another clue to his wife's true feelings was that her face was suffused with hatred every time she looked in his direction. All the same, he told himself, she was still an attractive woman. She had a lovely unhealthy pallor that still excited him a couple of times a month.

He turned his attention to his children – Lily, eight, and Hemlock, five.

'So, what you kids do at school today – anythink interestin'?'

Lily scowled and said, 'We 'ad to cut up a frog, but by the time it got to me the cowin' knife was blunt.' Hemlock said nothing. His bedroom was directly above the embalming room and the formaldehyde fumes seeping through the ceiling had withered his brain and subsequently his vocabulary. He communicated in grunts and aggressive physical movements. He had never been seen to smile. His parents were proud of him.

'I got a book out of the library last week,' said Mrs Doom. 'It was written by a woman called Germaine Greer.'

'Oh, yes,' said Mr Doom, absent-mindedly, his thoughts turning to working on his next body which lay on the slab beyond the connecting door.

'It's called *The Female Eunuch*,' continued Mrs Doom. 'I picked it up because it had a beautiful picture on the cover. A woman's torso, hanging from a hook.'

'Very nice,' agreed Mr Doom. What was all this leading to, he wondered. They never discussed literary matters at the table or elsewhere, for that matter.

'According to Germaine,' went on Mrs Doom, 'women are as good as men.'

This was news to Mr Doom, who didn't count a single

MR DOOM
the undertaker

MRS DOOM
the undertaker's wife

MISS DOOM
the undertaker's daughter

MASTER DOOM
the undertaker's son

woman undertaker amongst his acquaintance.

'So,' said Mrs Doom, 'I want to learn the trade. I want to pick the corpses up in the van. I want to embalm 'em. I want to arrange 'em in their cowin' coffins and I want to see 'em to their bleedin' graves.'

Mr Doom hadn't been so shocked since a cadaver had sat up on its slab and asked him for a cigarette.

Mrs Doom said, 'I'm sick of doin' the food for the funeral teas an' comfortin' the cowin' bereaved. I want to be a *proper* undertaker – like you.'

Mr Doom sipped at his tea; he needed a moment to think. His wife's proposition was ludicrous, of course. Mrs Doom must be embarking on The Change, that dreaded time of life when women went off their heads and left home to join the circus, or ran amok with a carving knife.

'Well, Doom?' She was on her feet, glowering at him from the scullery doorway. 'I need to know now, this *minute*,' she insisted, 'before I bring the cake in.'

Mr Doom said, 'Women are not suited to the work, Mrs D. They've got more – well, sensitive natures.'

'So,' she said murderously. 'No is your answer, is it?'

'Yes,' he said, 'no,' though he quaked internally at the ferocity of her tone. She went into the scullery and returned with an extravagantly decorated chocolate cake. Hemlock grunted his approval and Lily, unused to such teatime treats, asked, 'What's that?'

'It's called "Death by Chocolate",' smiled Mrs Doom, as she cut her husband a large and succulent slice.

Sue Townsend

THE ROCKS

Pictures by Barry Fantoni

Mr Rock the musician

Can you tell us, first of all, about your early influences?

Yeah. When I started playing, that was, like, in the early sixties when I was still at school. There were two roads you could go down. Some of the guys went down the Hank Marvin road, you know, playing 'Apache' and 'Wonderful Land' and doing the little dance steps.

But when did you start to get into the blues?

I've always been something of an individualist, you know. I realised from the first that if I was going to make my mark I was going to have to go my own way. So I got heavily into C. Paul Herfurth.

Herfurth . . . ?

He was a sort of guru of mine. He wrote this amazing book called *A Tune a Day for the Guitar* which really turned my head round. He introduced me to all sorts of stuff the rest of the kids just didn't know about. Really ahead of his time.

What sort of thing?

You know, stuff like 'Camptown Races' and 'Polly Wolly Doodle' and 'Silent Night' and 'Michael Row the Boat Ashore'. It can be pretty challenging, because if you do it right you sometimes have to change from a C chord to an F chord without stopping.

You were in a band at school?

Ha ha! Yeah. There were some guys at school who had a band and I'd only been playing a couple of weeks when they asked me to join.

Why was that?

Well, essentially it was a pretty free and easy time when

90

MR ROCK
the musician

MRS ROCK
the musician's wife

MASTER ROCK
the musician's son

ROCKS

MISS ROCK
the musician's daughter

attitude and image were as important as ability. I guess I had the right attitude and image. Yeah, it was attitude, image, and the fact that my dad was rich and bought them a Ford Transit van. The band broke up not long after I joined. Shortly after that they re-formed, but didn't ask me to join. I guess maybe my attitude was just a little too wild for them.

They kept the van, though?

Er . . . yeah.

You've always been seen as a seminal influence on many of the great bands of the sixties and seventies. Can you tell us about your work with The Who?

Yeah, this was back around 1963. They were called the High Numbers then. They were doing a gig at Eel Pie Island and I got talking to them after the gig and mentioned that I played the guitar and, you know, at first we didn't seem to have much in common – they were still into the blues and that sort of thing and I was onto the C. Paul Herfurth stuff. But then they mentioned that they needed a van and I mentioned that I'd got a lot of money, and the next thing I was in the band.

You went on tour together?

Yeah. All over. We must have hit every branch of Currie Motors in the West London area. Then up to Leo Macari's music shop in Charing Cross Road to fill the Transit up with new gear. Then they said they'd go and park the van and meet me in this café on Denmark Street. Next time I saw them was on *Ready Steady Go*. I think, in retrospect, the split was better for all of us. The musical differences went pretty deep. Pete Townsend wasn't really writing the sort of music I wanted to play.

Which was?

You know, 'Polly Woddle Doodle' and 'Michael Row the Boat Ashore'. The split was very amicable, though. They laughed

95

ever such a lot. It was that sort of good-time atmosphere.

You had pretty much the same influence on the early development of the Rolling Stones?

That was different. With the Stones it was much more volatile. Long rap sessions. Heavy stuff. I remember we were all up three nights in a row, just rapping and rowing about what direction the band ought to take. Bill Wyman wanted a VW Campervan, you see, but eventually I persuaded them they'd be better off with a Transit. The rest is history. Then I went to the States and worked with Dylan at Woodstock.

At the Woodstock Festival?

No. Trustee Eddie's English Fords, Best Valu on Highway 212.

Can we talk about your new album, '60s Hits'?

The thing I'm most proud about with this album is that it's an industry first. The single biggest advance that a record company has received from an artist for a one-album deal.

Can I have my van now?

Sure.

Mrs Rock the musician's wife

How did you and Andy meet?

Through Jimi Hendrix. I went round to Jimi's dressing room after a gig and we were, you know, talking, and suddenly Elvis Presley bursts in and said I was his girl. At this time Elvis was mainlining a cocktail of Quinoped and Burinex because he'd got really paranoid about getting athlete's foot in his kidneys. Anyway, Jimi was cool about it and offered to sell me to Elvis for 17s 6d. So Elvis gave him a quid and we went out to his car and we were driving away when Elvis suddenly realised that Jimi hadn't given him his change. So we went back and Elvis started breaking up Jimi's dressing room and shouting, 'Where's my goddam half crown, man?' Then Andy came in and gave 'em a Transit each, so I went home with him. Not long after that the eating disorders started.

What kind of eating disorders?

Comfort eating. It got so I could clear out a fridge at one sitting then start on the chrome trim and pipework. I knew I was out of control and had to get help.

You saw a psychiatrist?

I joined a Women's Consciousness Raising Group and they told me the reason I was so fat was because I was oppressed.

And knowing that helped get your eating under control?

No, it just made me bloody angry. I was fat and angry, and well on the way to an early coronary. Then in the mid-seventies I got into this very mystic thing and travelled to India to stay on an Ashram with Bagwhan Ron Presswell, who's this incredibly wise holy man with a figure like a biro refill. And he introduced me to what is probably the greatest personal discovery in my journey through life.

What was that?

Liposuction. You know, after a heavy session of meditating, Bagwhan Ron'd be tucking into the Mars bars, so I asked him what was the secret of his trim figure and he introduced me to Dr Gottblatt and his magic vac. One session and I had enough spare skin hanging off me to carpet a bedsit.

Has being slimmer improved your relationship with Andy?

Well . . . he's always been good to me. D'you want to see my vans?

Master Rock the musician's son

Could you describe your current set-up?

Yeah, right now I'm working with a Roland A80 mother keyboard MIDIed to a bank of Akai S1000 HDs plus one or two bits and bobs – a Yam SY77, couple of Ensoniq SD1s, Korg 01 and so on – all patched through a Macintosh running Cu-Base and mixing and mastering digitally in 32 track on another Mac hooked up to Digidesign's Pro-Tools; and all that's contained within the environment of a one-ton Transit with a Luton body, a customised automatic gearbox and ALB.

Do you find that the use of such a hi-tech set-up releases creative potential or do you experience problems interfacing with the equipment?

Er . . . parking's a bitch.

Miss Rock the musician's daughter

How does it feel to be the daughter of a famous rock star?

Is this Daddy's new record? Oh, golly, how sick-making. Listen, did Daddy send you? Just tell him, will you, I don't love him, I never have loved him and I never will love him. So he can just send some people round and get all those Transits out of the dorm. All right?

David Stafford

THE GRAPES

Pictures by Larry

The great advantage fiction-writing wallahs have over us reporters is that they can make the whole bally thing up. In no time they can knock out entire conversations to bring alive the Grapes family and their grudging line of bad-tempered public service. We reporters have to go out with a notebook in all weathers (rain, hail, sleet, you name it) and anything we write must be a bold upright fact that can stare you in the eyeball and be proud of itself.

And yet we do have one advantage over our fiction-writing brothers and sisters. They are ultimately constrained by the limits of the human imagination. We fact-merchants, by contrast, have free access to the wild world of everyday reality.

The first task was to find out about Mrs Grapes. It was while researching this good woman that I stumbled upon the Traffic Warden Support Group. Apparently morale was so low among London's 2,000 meter maids that a very nice man called Mr Pratley was brought in not long ago to run encounter groups that would give traffic wardens renewed belief in themselves. No one could invent this.

The life of the traffic warden sounded a nightmare. When the Metropolitan Police set up the first-ever squad of them in 1960 the recruits were all ex-army types. The result was that they brought far too much discipline to the simple task of putting tickets on parked cars. They had not one fat rule book, but two; and the rules were petty in the extreme.

There were 278 supervisors, controllers, senior controllers and area controllers in charge of a mere 2,000 'basic grade wardens'. The supervisors enforced their rule books with a vigour that gave the poor traffic wardens a miserable life. It is no wonder they passed this irritable officiousness on to us, the offending motorists.

The wardens were not allowed to work in pairs or to have long hair dangling beneath their hats. They were barred from entering banks, shops or private homes because the supervisors did not want people slipping them fivers.

All wardens carried a pocket book into which they had to enter every detail of their day, including the exact moment when they entered the lavatory and left it; the supervisors spent their time patrolling round the beats checking up on them. They had to sign the warden's book every time they saw them. This could be as often as four times a day. No wonder the poor meter maids did not feel trusted.

Further, the rules demanded that wardens had to carry round a hated and heavy shoulder bag packed to the gunwales with things like torches, pac-a-macs and fluorescent jackets; and for all this, plus public loathing and walking several thousand miles a year, the wardens were paid a salary of £7,000.

In the eighteen months before the encounter group sessions, half the traffic wardens in London resigned. No wonder Mrs Grapes looks cheesed off. But I have to report that a subtle blend of Mrs Thatcher and Mr Pratley has changed all that.

Two years ago Mrs Thatcher's think tank turned its attention to traffic wardens and found ninety-nine ways of improving the meter maid's lot. It was like a bomb going off. Their report called for better pay, more responsibility, the scrapping of senior controllers and supervisors and the complete rewriting of the rule books to give scope for personal initiative to wardens who would no longer be described as 'basic'.

MR 'SOUR' GRAPES
the VAT inspector

MRS GRAPES
the VAT inspector's wife

MISS GRAPES
the VAT inspector's daughter

MASTER GRAPES
the VAT inspector's son

The mundane meter work is now being taken over by local authorities and the wardens themselves have been promoted – to clamping. What is more, they are to be given new, improved 'bum bags' to strap around their waists and take the weight off their shoulders. It is a revolution.

This is where Mr Pratley came in with his 'hearts and minds' seminars for traffic wardens. He arranged for every warden in London to spend a day in plain clothes 'relating to colleagues'. Chiefs and Indians sat eyeball to eyeball, expressing their points of view. They were told to voice their fears, anxieties and dissatisfactions. Old barriers were broken down and the militaristic era of rules and suspicion was swept aside. The hope now is that the scowl will disappear from Mrs Grapes' face.

The next task was to find Mr Grapes. You would not believe the conversations I have had with various personnel departments trying to find a VAT inspector who is married to a traffic warden.

'Why do you want to know?' they said.

'Because I want to inquire about their general contentment as a family unit.'

'Why?'

(Long explanation about fund-raising books, children's charities, Romanian hospitals, the whole popularity of Happy Families cards in the postwar period.)

And after all this I have to inform you that, so far as anybody is aware, no VAT inspector on this planet is in a state of wedlock (happy or otherwise) with any known traffic warden. Such a coupling only occurs, it seems, in the fevered imagination of a cartoonist.

Stephen Pile

105

THE GREEDS

Pictures by Charles Griffin

Approaching the end of a long and engrossing business career, Mr Greed is nearly ubiquitous. An urban redevelopment scheme requiring commercial sponsorship? A famous football club fallen on evil days? A politician needing moral counsel? Mr Greed is your man. He will administer a six-figure cheque to a charity and a rebuke to the leader of the Labour Party with the same air of calculated insouciance. Borne aloft on a tide of highly publicised interventions, he will demand only that he receive the recognition and approbation which he has always assumed to be the philanthropist's due. In consequence, Mr Greed is a conspicuous figure on the frail, luridly-lit catwalk of public life.

Curiously, the limelight which suffuses Mr Greed's public persona – what Mr Greed, ever the most modish of men, would call his 'image' – coexists with an unprecedented degree of commercial stealth. Mr Greed's reputation, cultivated it must be said by himself, is that of a highly successful self-made entrepreneur, but the shrewdest young city gentleman who ever inhabited an office in Leadenhall Street would be hard put to say of what precisely it is that his business consists. There are gloomy premises in Finsbury Square, manned by the most punctilious commissionaire in all London; there is a holding company, Greed Holdings, with offices nobody quite knows where; there are musty cobwebs of data in Companies House, each leading back to domiciles in Vaduz, Liechtenstein and Grand Canary. The impressive array of statistics which annually bedazzles his shareholders has never quite dissipated this air of mystery.

MR GREED
the financier

MISS GREED
the financier's daughter

MASTER GREED
the financier's son

MRS GREED
the financier's wife

Mr Greed's soccer team parades in shirts proclaiming the message 'We Need Greed' – a slogan of Mr Greed's own devising – but nobody has satisfactorily determined what it is that we need Mr Greed for, or where exactly we might find him.

This aura of concealment, reserve maybe, extends to Mr Greed's early life. His celebrity is of recent date, his progress through the twilit landscape of the immediately postwar era unremarked and undocumented. The tabloid newspapers, which at one time or another took out and examined his personal history in a rather wistful way, were able to establish only that he had stood for parliament at the General Election of 1959 in the Mosleyite interest (Mr Greed has since repudiated what he calls 'this youthful folly'; he is a notable friend of Israel). The rest was the airiest speculation, the merest fancy: Central European parentage, glamorous clandestine war service. Such was Mr Greed's amusement at this litany of invention that he withheld his customary writ.

The truth, though prosaic, is not without interest as an example of personal tenacity harnessed to propitious circumstance. Humbly born – his father was an emigré stevedore at the East India dock – cast out into the world with little except an invincible faith in his own abilities, George Greed was one of the original hard-faced men who did well out of the war. Its conclusion found him in possession of a defunct printing works in Hoxton, five hundred grey herringbone suits and a quantity of contraband chocolate bars. The hour found the man, the man found an alias – Mr Greed's baptismal name is polysyllabic and vowel-less – and a series of stalls in the street markets of the East End.

From Brick Lane to the Lord Mayor's Banquet is not perhaps too startling a progress in these fluid times. Mr Greed's career has been marked, on the one hand, by a strong instinct for self-preservation and, on the other, by an extraordinary ability to predict the commercial future. The one allowed him to prophesy accurately which of his hitherto useful business acquaintances might subsequently become outright liabilities (he lent money to Peter Rachman, knew Jim Slater when the latter was a clerk); the other prompted him to renew the works at Hoxton in time to take advantage of the magazine boom of the early sixties. By the time of the first Wilson government he was making up the plates for the *Radio Times*, a fact of which the BBC remained ignorant. But it was municipal socialism that sealed Mr Greed's destiny. Scarcely a tower block rose to dominate the blitzed alleyways of Bermondsey and Poplar without Mr Greed having a hand in its construction. The buildings are great empty shells now, and Mr Greed a proponent of the property-owning democracy; but there is, as he himself has pointed out, such a thing as historical inevitability.

With his seventieth birthday approaching – the call from the Palace can surely not be much longer delayed – Mr Greed appears invulnerable. If there is a chink in his expansive carapace it lies in his family. There are other Greeds, variously at large in the byways of our national life, but they are sluggish rivulets when set against the fount from which they flow. Such is the lustre of Mr Greed's own personality that those close to him have an unfortunate habit of being extinguished by it. Nothing else, surely, could explain how an expensive education and prolonged parental exhortation could yet produce such offspring as Keith and Jasmine Greed. It is in the company of his family, too, that Mr Greed's customary decisiveness deserts him. He cannot admit his son and daughter wholly into his counsels, nor can he bring himself unreservedly to exclude them. This combination of indulgence and asperity is congenial neither to

Mr Greed's own peace of mind nor to the administration of Greed Holdings. Mrs Greed, for her part, inhabits an hotel near St Tropez where she is famously rude to waiters.

If Mr Greed – pictured at a charity sporting event or stepping in to save yet another beleaguered national institution – is troubled by these seeds of doubt, he does not show it. After all, many great empires have died with their creators, and Mr Greed is wise enough to know that the weakness of his heirs, along with other, unspecified factors, will see an end to it all. Until that time he is content to continue along the path of what he himself regards as public service – and which only a hostile newspaper would describe as self-advertisement. An overweening consciousness of his own rectitude was ever the touchstone of Mr Greed's career. Posterity may consider him less kindly.

D. J. Taylor

THE GLOODS

Pictures by Lucy Willis

Imagine my surprise when I read recently that a consortium of Independent Television Broadcasters had appointed my old friend Rodney Glood from Cambridge University as their scheduling supremo. Glood, in future, would be the sole judge of what we would see on ITV.

At Magdalene, the duffer's college (they threw you a rugger ball and if you caught it they let you in; if you threw it back they gave you a scholarship), Glood had stood out uniquely as something of an egghead. A fat and bookish boy, he had locked himself away in his room – 'sporting your oak' we called it – reading Wittgenstein and Leavis, eventually achieving first class honours and, rather to our surprise – since such employment did little justice to his intellect – securing a job in industry working for Metal Box.

That was the last I heard or saw of him – until I read that he had become the ITV supremo. That seemed odd, I thought. Why would a crew of fat businessmen in suits appoint as their supremo an artsy-fartsy, head-in-the-clouds intellectual who wouldn't know Jeremy Beadle from a sack of meal? Like any good journalist I sniffed a story here and I made it my business to seek him out, soon learning that he now lived as a recluse in Slough with Elsie, his wife, and their two children Jasper, eight, and Tracey, three.

Before you could say Robert Robinson, and with reporter's notebook at the ready, I found myself in Slough, where I recognised his house in no time (an unpleasant semi-detached in a suburban avenue) by dint of the fact that it had enough smart technology on its roof – dishes, aerials and so forth – to land Concorde in a fog. An announcement pinned

MR GLOOD
the TV addict

MRS GLOOD
the TV addict's wife

MASTER GLOOD
the TV addict's son

MISS GLOOD
the TV addict's daughter

to the front said: 'Kindly let yourself in and make your own way to the viewing lounge.'

I followed the instruction, shortly discovering the reason for it. My old friend Rodney had always been fat but now he was the size of the European butter mountain. Nor did his wife Elsie lose much by comparison: Mr and Mrs were both so heroically fat that they would not have been able to get to the front door even if they'd wanted to.

'Good to see you again,' said Rodney, without taking his eyes off the screen. 'I expect you want to interview me about my new job. Kindly keep your questions short and confine them to the commercial breaks.'

I waited for ten minutes, at which point an Australian afternoon melodrama was replaced by some monkeys selling tea.

'How did you get like this?' I said.

'Like what?'

'A television addict. A potato-brain.'

'I was fortunate, I suppose.'

'But you used to be so clever.'

'Clever, yes,' said Rodney, 'but I didn't know anything, did I? Now I know everything. Ask me a question.'

'How, during a heatwave, could you express the net probability that everyone will have a bath at the same time?'

'Mathematics, is it?' said Rodney. 'Probability theory and so forth? Not my department. I do Sue Lawley, threatened species, chat shows, *The Sky at Night*, dolphins, Japanese films, cooking, gardening, Brazil, Jonathon Ross and sport. You'll have to address your questions to Tracey. She has six degrees from the Open University. Chemistry, American literature, comparative religions, astrophysics, metallurgy and mathematical logic. Plus she does chess, bridge and Spanish dancing. Tracey?'

'The total net probability of everyone taking a bath during a water shortage is $V = pl(a-f(1) + p2(2a-f(2) + ..pn(na-f(n))$. Pass the crisps.'

'What about Esther Rantzen?' I asked.

'What about her?' said Tracey.

'Who does her?'

'No one does her,' said Tracey. 'We haven't lost all sense of proportion here.'

I was impressed. I waited for the next commercial break and then probed for some background material.

'When I last saw you,' I said to Glood, 'you were about to start work for Metal Box. How long did that last?'

'Two days,' said Glood. 'More accurately, the same day twice. Then the Chairman asked me to a dinner party. "Will Kojak be there?" I said. "No," he said. I was amazed. Why did this fool think that his dinner party, on which his common wife might have spent £43.23 including wine, could compete in the schedules with a TV series on which America's finest creative talents had spent millions of dollars? I never left the house again.'

'How have you been paying for the crisps and so forth?'

'I started entering "This Week's Clanger" competitions in the tabloids. In *Minder* on Monday, Her Indoors wore six curlers in one shot, but in the next she only had five! That was worth £10. Plus I became adept at general knowledge quizzes on cereal packets. Then young Michael Grade asked me to advise on scheduling. He was out and about too much. Didn't know enough. Couldn't spot the clangers. Too many power breakfasts with other ignorant men. It seems I have a knack for it – hence my new job as ITV supremo.'

We're in good hands – in so far, at least, as we'll be seeing less of Esther Rantzen.

William Donaldson

THE FAXES
Pictures by Matt

Felicity Fax cannot quite believe that she once wrote poems. Sometimes, when sorting out the Rexel display files in her study, she comes across old photographs and other relics of that former self who reclined in punts reciting Yeats while bespectacled Basil Biro, the lad that most pleasured her of all that with her lay, punted her gently down the Cam. But it was her winsome way with words that landed her, in 1967, the kind of job everyone wanted: creative copywriter with Medlicott Magdalene Monck (later MMMF, when Fax was added) the most dashing advertising agency of the day.

Mrs Fax is now forty-five and on the board. ('Girls used to have to be good in the bedroom – now they're good in the boardroom,' as she said in her opening address to the Women in Management conference.) She who once wore an Afghan kaftan and flowers in her flowing hair now has power shoulders on her pinstripe Armani and a laptop computer in her slimline briefcase and cannot imagine life without the carphone in her BMW, which keeps her in touch with husband (the same Basil Biro, but now known to all as Mr Fax) and their children Fanny and Freddie, at home. When her career began, there were long languid lunches in trattorie and whole afternoons in which to create dreamy slogans like 'Yoghurt is quite nice . . . sometimes' which won her her first award. Now she leaves home at dawn, lunches briskly in New York and Concordes back for dinner meetings with MMMF clients.

Mrs Fax has been the breadwinner of the family since Mr Fax became redundant. (Never having used her married name, she insisted that the children should be called Fax-

Biro, but everyone agrees it is simpler if they are all called Fax.) People say in jest, 'Do the Faxes have fax?' and the Faxes chorus, 'Do we ever!' There are four facsimile machines in the Faxhole, their quaintly named house in a leafy Georgian corner of Islington. There are also several laser printers and a dot-matrix, a modem and the last word in PBX telephone systems ('The President') and two full-size computers. There is 'a time-management facility in every other room,' as Mr Fax likes to say, 'or clock, to you.'

Basil stays at home these days, a househusband, since his own job as an arts administrator – once a lucrative and glamorous post – was cut in the Cuts of the 80s, though Basil's legacy of municipally-funded murals on all the borough's bottle-banks remains a visible reminder of his former power. He has got used to being the only person of the male persuasion collecting children at the school gates. Plenty of men deliver, he notices, but they are all in city suits, about to make their escape; his corduroy trousers are alone among the dirndl-skirts at 3.10 and 3.35, the awkwardly disparate coming-out times of Freddie and Fanny respectively. (At PTA meetings he pleads eloquently for some rationalisation of these times, but gets no support from the mums who seem to relish the extra wait, for their inexhaustible chats.)

Does Basil work? people ask, as if a household could run itself, with only Mrs Duster doing her slow-motion hoovering for two hours each morning. He has come to realise that the demands of househusbandry – chauffeuring to swimming and piano lessons, weekly birthday parties, choir practice and Saturday morning soccer, the daily packed lunches, the finding of games equipment and making instant costumes ('Fanny has been chosen to be Fairy Fantasia: please make a pair of wings and a starry headdress'), the fish fingers and shepherd's pie and the reading aloud from *James*

MRS FAX
the account executive

MR FAX
the account executive's husband

MISS FAX
the account executive's daughter

MASTER FAX
the account executive's son

and the Giant Peach and *Anne of Green Gables* until he falls, hallucinating, asleep, in the nursery armchair – need more intensive administrating than Islington's arts ever did.

Friends of the little Faxes think Freddie and Fanny must be the luckiest kids they know. They never see Mrs Fax at all (she is never home before bedtime) and Mr Fax never shouts at them to turn off the telly and come and have tea. And they have this amazing video-game library, with Super Nintendo and Sega Megadrive and portable Sega Game Gear. Fanny was the first child in the neighbourhood to get into level three in Super Mario, in Shinobi and Thunderblade. But while Miss Fax is her mother's daughter, rarely without a cellphone in her ear, even while riding her tricycle, Master Fax shows signs of being an old-fashioned child. Like his dad, he prefers his train set. And when offered a Scalextric he said what he really liked playing with best was his dad's old Meccano set and his grandfather's hoop and stick. Mrs Fax, when told of this, got on her cellphone at once to her clients, Toys 2000.'Mega marketing idea. Retro-toys. We'll handle the campaign . . . .'

Valerie Grove

THE ACRES

Pictures by Sue Macartney-Snape

The Earl of Acre the landowner

Until 1986 the 14th Earl of Acre lived quietly in Northamptonshire as plain Sir Dingleigh Dell, Bt. He was suddenly called upon to succeed to the earldom after a meteorite landed on the ballroom of Coppice (pron. Copse) Hall and wiped out the 13th Earl and forty-seven of his closest relations, celebrating the then Earl's fifth wedding.

Sir Dingleigh, educ. Uppingham, b. 1920, joined the army in 1939, giving his occupation as 'staying with people'. He had a distinguished career in the Catering Corps. After he had commandeered the contents of an Indian spice boat, his Pemmican-and-Hard-Tack Curry became a byword in Italy and North Africa. He was decorated with the DSO after an act of outstanding courage at Monte Cassino when he rescued the regiment's food supplies in the teeth of enemy fire.

Decommissioned in 1946, he pursued a career in catering. He pioneered tea shops in stately homes and made a fortune selling quality fudge in gingham bags. His company, 'Knobs', provided first class catering to the gentry. Indeed, it was because of 'Knobs' that he inherited his title; as forty-eighth in line to the 13th Earl, he was the natural choice as caterer for his wedding reception. Thus it happened that at the precise moment of meteoric impact Sir Dingleigh was pacing anxiously at the back gate, waiting the long overdue arrival of the pavlovas. Sadly, they arrived too late for the guests to enjoy them.

Since becoming Earl, he has continued to administer his catering empire. He has turned Coppice Hall from a white

THE EARL OF ACRE
the landowner

THE COUNTESS OF ACRE
the landowner's wife

CEDRIC, VISCOUNT FFIELD
the landowner's son

ACRES

LADY HECTARIA FFIELD
the landowner's daughter

elephant into a highly profitable business, constantly expanding and developing new exhibits. The Wedding Ballroom Memorial is a much visited showpiece on the estate. Coppice Toffee, Coppice Lollies and Coppice Jujubes are all brand leaders in stately homes' outlets.

His hobby is 'shooting anything one can eat'.

The Countess of Acre the landowner's wife

It is hard to imagine, when viewing the corpulent frame of the Countess, that she was once Beryl Beaumont, the celebrated showgirl who rose to prominence after winning the coveted title, Miss Holiday Guest House 1948. (Her parents were the proprietors of Fayre Glaydes, a popular twenty-one-bedroom hotel in Southsea.) Her rise to stardom was swift.

It was as Babette, the French maid in *Fun in the Army*, that she caught the eye of the young Dingleigh Dell seated in D7. He took her to the Ritz, he took her to the Savoy, but it was over a slice of walnut cake at Fuller's Café that he proposed two weeks later.

After their marriage, the Countess retired from the spotlight. Nowadays, little remains of her youthful showbiz glamour; an occasional flash of the eye, a song at the piano after dinner, a tendency to overdress.

Her days are occupied in charitable works and acquiring farms. Recently, she appeared in a BBC2 *Forty Minutes* documentary, 'Dukes, Earls and Dancing Girls', and has been swamped with offers to return to the stage. She remains obdurate, however, preferring to spend her days examining the minutiae of genetic engineering and Set Aside. She is much loved by her staff and the locals, who overlook minor eccentricities such as sleeping in her tiara and a fondness for 100 per cent proof peppermint liqueur.

Cedric, Viscount ffield, the landowner's son

Behind the somewhat etiolated appearance of Cedric, Viscount ffield (b. 1950), lies both a formidable intellect and a razor-sharp business mind. Whilst his stammer and lisp made him an object of ridicule as a boy (his short left leg and his lack of hand-eye coordination left him defenceless at the Wall Game), he was an outstanding King's Scholar at Eton where he was known as 'Swotty Dell'. He went to Peterhouse College, Cambridge, where he gained a double first in Russian and Polish, quoting his mother's favourite saying, 'You'll be sure to want them later.'

He then spent several years with one of the major international auction houses. He has put the knowledge gained there to spectacularly good use. He picked up a few nice bits of china at Mentmore, for instance, and a number of old masters from Althorp are said to hang in the private library at Coppice Hall. Since becoming Viscount ffield he is often to be seen bidding at the liquidation and bankruptcy sales of former schoolmates.

During the early years of *perestroika* and *glasnost* he made a number of important contacts in Eastern Europe, ferreting out old White Russian families who would happily exchange ancient artefacts for dollars. After the destruction of the Berlin Wall things became easier, and he now has a fleet of lorries that takes out vast shipments of Coppice Toffee to all parts of the old Soviet Union, bringing back vanloads of long-case clocks.

In 1989, he married Sikha, the beautiful Tahitian supermodel. They live in the dower house at Coppice, and have two children, Dingleigh Junior and Poppy. Cedric rarely sees his sister.

Lady Hectaria ffield the landowner's daughter

On spotting Hez, as Lady Hectaria ffield is known amongst friends, one would never guess that she was a member of the aristocracy, as she is very much an everyday 'girl about town'. Born in 1952, she attended a surprisingly large number of top private girls' boarding schools in what seems to have been an educational experiment. She went missing from Benenden at the age of sixteen and was discovered later in Berlin where she was improving her German (she shares her brother's gift for languages) and acting as road manager to a female impersonator known as Liebchen.

Her parents decided then that A-levels were not for Hectaria, and so she applied successfully for the Stage Management Course at the London Academy of Music and Dramatic Art. She excelled in electrics, and her half-hour calls over the tannoy were particularly enjoyed by the acting students due to the mellifluous beauty of her speaking voice.

Her early working life was spent in fringe theatre as Company Manager for a number of leading womens' theatre groups: Red Stain, eFemera, Bondage Theatrix and the Clock Off and Sign On Theatre Company. In the last few years she has emerged as one of our leading lighting designers, and crosses Europe regularly on her 1962 1,000 cc Harley Davidson, travelling between the great theatres of Paris, Hamburg, Vienna and London.

She has shared a large house in fashionable Hackney for many years with her flatmate, the well-known society masseuse Gigi Dutton, who numbers many of our top actresses among her clients. They mix in an amusing circle of theatrical and artistic folk, and are often to be seen at the Groucho Club.

Lady Hectaria shows little sign of getting married, but her parents have not given up hope.

Dillie Keane

THE TRIPS

Pictures by Gray Jolliffe

Mr Trip the time-traveller

Mr Trip lives quietly in 'Traveller's Rest' with his family: Mrs Trip, Master Trip and Miss Trip. He is often away on business, sometimes for months on end. Mrs Trip (Honoria) worries about him; and so, to a lesser extent, do the children, who have both watched all the old videos of *Dr Who* and know that in a corner of the garage stands the original Time Machine. Mrs Trip thinks he may be up to something when he's away from home. Once, from the H. G. Wells band of the Future, he brought back an attractive young woman called Lydia. Though he explained to Mrs Trip that she was one of the Eloi, a caste of the Future dedicated to harmlessness and fooling about, she took it badly. Lydia now works for the family as a sort of *au pair*.

On another occasion, from the same time band, Mr Trip brought back a young morlock. The children are very fond of him and he is their only family pet. His behaviour alienated the cat, who has not been seen since he arrived.

The Trip children, Dylan and Maureen, are always agitating for their father to bring back a dinosaur. Indeed, he did once promise to bring back a dinosaur's egg for Easter. As for the dinosaur itself, 'It isn't easy,' he says. Mr Trip often complains that he feels he was born before his Time. 'Ahead of his Time' is another phrase he uses. He has been known to call his mother-in-law 'that old stegosaurus'.

In spite of his interest in the Future, Mr Trip sometimes speaks with real nostalgia of the Ancient World. When questioned about Roman orgies under the Emperors, he will exclaim, 'Those were the days!' and a dreamy

MR TRIP
the time-traveller

MASTER TRIP
the time-traveller's father

MISS EINSTEIN
the time-traveller's mother

MRS TRIP
the time-traveller's wife

look comes into his eyes.

He has often been asked by the children if he couldn't take them too. His answer, so far, has been that there isn't really room in the Time Machine – and particularly not if he's going to be loaded up with sabre-toothed tigers (one of Dylan's requests) and the like. Mrs Trip, who is unadventurous, has shown no desire to accompany him and Mr Trip seems satisfied with this. To the neighbours Mrs Trip says, significantly, 'You know what travellers are.' Nevertheless Mr Trip has hinted that he may one day build a new enlarged version of the Time Machine, which now looks very Late Victorian – being, at the time of writing, nearly a hundred years old. It was built in 1894, as he reminds his cronies in the Dog and Duck, in the days when the Old Master was alive . . . .

Mr Trip the time-traveller

Whizzing through Time
can be quite sublime –
some of the people can be very nice,
but others you wouldn't look at twice.

Mrs Trip the time-traveller's wife

This can't last!
He doesn't know if he's
in the Future or the Past!
You can't call me fussy
if I don't trust him –
I think he's up to something
with some brazen Neolithic hussy!

Miss Einstein the time-traveller's mother

I like to go back to see our Mam
when she was in her pram!
I like bending Time and Space –
and, in a way, it puts her in her place!

Master Trip the time-traveller's father

When I travel back to see my Dad
I think 'What a very ordinary lad!'
But some inventive talent there must have
    been,
or he couldn't have built that
very clever machine!

Gavin Ewart

THE NEMOS

Pictures by Quentin Blake

Mr Nemo the master of disguise

Mr Nemo is thirty-seven, not a great age for a man but fairly elderly for a vacuum cleaner. His father was a Hebridean illusionist, specialising in tartan vanishes and filling the stage with heather. His mother was small and ineffectual, and was once claimed as a prize in a bran-tub.

Mr Nemo first became interested in disguise at a children's party when, falling asleep in a gaudy pullover, he was mistaken for a length of lino. He enjoyed the subsequent congratulations and attention, and the blancmange he was given to take home as a reward enabled the family to eat well for twenty minutes.

He then determined on a career in show business and left school at the age of sixteen intending to pursue a B Tech qualification in Quick Change and Misdirection at Kidderminster Poly. Unfortunately, travelling to the Midlands on a coach with no lavatory facilities, he trapped an individual part of his anatomy in a small thermos, and had to be admitted to the Casualty Department of an outmoded hospital.

Whilst convalescing outside the main boiler room, Mr Nemo met the man who was to pass on the secret skills of the disguise professional. Mr Nemo did not appreciate the significance of that first meeting; mistaking the old master for a portable television, he did not embark on a conversation, but merely concentrated on improving the reception for *Take the High Road*. This hilarious incident was later worked up into a full-blown anecdote and, with the addition of punctuation, became a radio situation comedy starring Molly Weir and Basil D'Oliveira.

The old master of disguise, whose health was failing, raced against time to pass on to Mr Nemo the tricks of his mysterious trade. Passing nurses would be puzzled by overheard remarks such as 'Now button it up' and 'Don't believe the textbooks, it will fold in two.'

One day the old man whispered to Mr Nemo that he had no more to teach him, lay back on his pillow and died. He was then taken to the laundry and ironed. Mr Nemo had walked into that hospital ward an ungainly immature adolescent, but he walked out a tea bag.

Mrs Nemo the master of disguise's wife

Mrs Nemo, or Vera as she prefers to be called, has never had any interest in disguise, and only engages in it reluctantly in the cause of family solidarity, subjugating her desires to those of her husband as a deliberate act of post-feminism.

Brought up in a leafy suburb of Manchester, she spent an idyllic adolescence snipping off her split ends with a Stanley knife and sending large padded valentines to Dave, Dozey, Beaky and Titch. She was never that keen on Mick.

Vera was unable to follow her chosen career as a hairstylist, owing to an inability to do a centre parting, and for a while she became very depressed, worrying her parents dreadfully by hanging around the back of the Free Trade Hall, hoping to exchange salacious badinage with the woodwind section of the Hallé Orchestra. She soon grew out of this rebellious stage, however, and settled down happily as a trainee travel agent, specialising in mystery tours to mundane locations.

It was while she was arranging for a Mr and Mrs Vitkunas to be taken two hundred miles by gypsy caravan to their own allotment, that she met Mr Nemo. He was leaning against a display of holiday brochures, thinking about alopecia, when

MR NEMO
the master of disguise

MRS NEMO
the master of disguise's wife

MISS NEMO
the master of disguise's daughter

MASTER NEMO
the master of disguise's son

he caught sight of Vera in her tie-neck blouse and jaunty blow-wave, and fell in love.

They were married in Didsbury Cathedral after an embarrassing altercation in the verger's washroom, Vera refusing to tie the knot as long as Mr Nemo was disguised as an oak veneer escritoire with slight scratching and reproduction fittings.

They honeymooned happily in Beirut (long before it became so crowded) spending their days sightseeing and their evenings teaching the hotel dog to pass himself off as a gas fitter.

Mrs Nemo now only disguises herself on business occasions, and is happiest spending her spare time in the local charity shop, writing '30p' in faint pencil on the fly leaves of books such as Agatha Christie's *They Do It with Mirrors* and *A Nurse in Action* by Evelyn Prentis.

Master Nemo the master of disguise's son

Master Nemo has been a sore trial to his parents from day one, when he sprang from the womb to a general cry of 'It's a toast rack!'

Now in his moody teenage years, he tends to rebel against his parents, attending family get-togethers in a collar and tie, and wearing school uniform at school.

He is not academically minded, and has only two low-grade GCSEs, both for shampooing. There is however a new City and Guilds Disguise and Catering course on offer in a nearby hamlet, and Master Nemo may be able to join this if he can muster the necessary pencil case.

He has a steady girlfriend, whose name he has never quite caught. She is a member of the British Winter Nudist Association, who meet regularly in damp woodland and get thoroughly miserable.

Miss Nemo the master of disguise's daughter

Miss Nemo, though of tender years, has her sights firmly set on a career in the spotlight. Her mother often remarks that she danced before she could talk, and very irritating it was too, having someone asking for the butter in tango.

She spends many hours on her appearance, and can often be found in the early hours, combing her leg hairs with precision-made surgical instruments, and varnishing her toenails with products only usually available to the motor industry.

A sweet-natured child, she often visits old folk, sometimes as herself and sometimes as an outsize squirrel in dungarees. This, she reckons, stimulates the elderly people, and helps them stave off low-grade viral infections.

Her ambition is to form a dance quartet with Michael Jackson, Dannii Minogue and Arnold Schwarzenegger. He may not be able to dance but he should have no trouble carrying the costumes up the fire escape.

Victoria Wood